Fictitiously Nonfiction

~repus

BookLeaf Publishing

India | USA | UK

Presentation by *BookLeaf Publishing*

Web: www.bookleafpub.com

E-mail: info@bookleafpub.com

ISBN: 9789360946241

First edition 2024

DEDICATION

This book is dedicated to every single person trying to live life while dealing with any form of psychological, physical, spiritual and/or substance abuse; I promise you are not alone. There are others of us out here doing the best we can to navigate through this thing we call life. Please do not ever feel afraid or scared to reach out for help, as it just may save your life; it has saved mine more than once.

This is also dedicated to everybody who has been, and still is, affected by the wildfires on Maui, HI, on Aug. 8th, 2023. My heart and soul perpetually break for every single person we continue to lose, for they may be gone, but will never be forgotten, and we will rebuild our community to honor them.

ACKNOWLEDGEMENT

Firstly, I would like to thank my senior year English teacher, Mrs. Dennis, as she saw a potential in me that I had not seen in myself, so she pushed me and I hated it at that time, but without that shove, I would not be writing this today. I am forever grateful for my friends and family who have provided me with constant support and inspiration over this lifetime, especially Lady Madonna, Princess Leia, Rhiannon Michelle, and of course, my main muse, Booty – I truly love you all more than I am able to express in words alone.

I would like to thank Ivy, Arushi, Lavleen and everyone else at BookLeaf Publishing for assisting me in making this collection of confusion in my head a reality, as I would not be able to consolidate this properly myself.

Lastly, as much as it hurts, I must thank those I have loved and lost in this lifetime; you left an impression on my soul, which inspires most of the blood that spills out of my pen when I put it to paper. I know we signed a contract with stardust before we began this cycle; not only do

I forgive you if I ever felt you hurt me, but more importantly, I sincerely apologize if I ever hurt you, because I do love you.

PREFACE

I have been writing as a therapeutic tool for most of my life, and it has literally saved my life many more times than once. Some things are safer and easier to jot down in a notebook than they are to say out loud, and if these words can help anyone else who is struggling out there, I feel like I'm doing my part for this gift with words that I have been given.

No one is perfect, period, and I sincerely believe rules are meant to bend at will, but for those of us that truly do not know the rules to begin with, we have another world of possibilities ahead of us. Some of the pieces included here are in all lowercase, but I pray that you do not let that distract you from the content, as it is all very relative.

To and Through

As I dream of tomorrow,
I'm full of anxiety;
When I think of the past,
It simply depresses me
Because I am not here
Living in this moment;
I'm all over the place,
So far from content.
Since I have been imbued,
Full of uncertainty;
Will tomorrow still be safe?
We just have to wait and see.

When that time comes along,
Cognizant memories;
Are these thoughts of something
Much more collectively?

For we are all one
In the same, just alike,
Clawing our way through this hell;
Praying that we just might
Make it out alive today,
Tomorrow, another chance.
Trying to be a better man

Than my previous existence;
So, please show me the light
And help me pave the way
To much better tomorrows,
Through much better todays.

They Come and They Go

Drifting thoughts
Floating back and forth,
Left and right,
Flowing endlessly
Through tides of change
In the seas of time
Always wash themselves
Back upon the
Shores
Of my
Mind.

Collecting debris
Along the way
While lowering
Visibility
During the pushing
And the pull
Of the current
And its undertow.

Producing
Vibrating waves of
Distraction
That continue to

Crash down on this
Constantly fading,
Short-term memory,
Eroding with every
Passing
Splash of
Thought.

to ashes, dust to

i'm here in the now and i'm not sure what to do
with myself in this life after all i've been through
full of pain and despair, from losing those i love,
to the fire, the destruction, but i'm looking up
above
to the skies, the clouds, whatever heaven may be
beyond the cosmos, all the stardust, all that
makes us we
to the core of my being and my spirituality
god, please help me get back to who i used to be
when i was a child and full of innocence
without a care in the world, and full of
confidence
tomorrow always comes, and there is no worry
when time does not exist, so there is no hurry
to make decisions when i know my head is not
clear -
i just need some time to get over my fears
of sirens, abrupt sounds and the smell of smoke;
my ptsd multiplied; i feel like i may choke
on the dust in the air and all of the toxicity
as they sift through the ashes of who we used to
be.

Who Needs a Dictionary?

The tears held back
in the eyes
just before breaking
the barrier,
the point in which
they drip down,
is the definition
of suspense.

Lacking

This morning, I didn't wake;
sleep slipped between the folds
that made me. Looking up
only proved to cauterize
these retinas; sun flares flashed
bright white light, blindness.
Pain seared through the membranes
that once contained sanity. Inane
thoughts cross this burnt-out mind.
Feeling the need, the urgency
to pass beyond this barrier
which holds back. Attacking
silently, quietly and effectively
this worn out will to weave
between the sheets and the creeps.
Daydreaming nightmares and
the inability to see beyond
the edge that we step upon.
Black and white fade to gray
as time is death measured depth,
or lack of perception; attention,
feeling cashed, I shall crash
into the oblivious nature
that left me alone, yet again.

the nth time

eye don't bleed anymore.
cut my wrist today, the nth time,
only crimson failed to spread
across my sea of azure; instead
words, no, letters, disjointed
and jumbled around, spilled in
place of what once was read.
now it is all misunderstood,
and eye fear the same
for myself; maybe eye just
need to cut a little deeper.

Excessive Moderation

I was staring at the hole
in my ruptured wall today
when I heard something
that made me want to enter.

I already know what's inside
but today I heard another voice,
an unfamiliar voice;
it was almost comforting
to listen to,
although it was a little unclear.
I just like
the way it sounded.

So I crawled inside my hole,
careful not to slip
through the cracks;
it was darker than before,
but I could see just fine.

Then I heard
that voice again,
as I saw someone
running away;
I wanted to chase them down
but I was told to stay:

"Do not turn around,
you know who I am;
take this dagger
and drink my wine,
then complete
this task at hand..."

So I waited
and I wondered
as I watched
and I pondered
while I drank
and I swallowed
until I saw him
and I followed
in the footsteps
of the shadow before me,
close enough,
but not to detect me,
to the place
I knew would be
the death of one
inside of me.

"Now" said the voice
that came from behind.
I wanted to turn and look
but it was not the right time,

so I dug the knife
straight into the heart
and it was all so perfect,
right from the start,
until he fell down
and looked up at me;
this is the person
that I was supposed to be,
surrounded in
a pool of blood
and lying dead
right before me.

So I turned around to find
that the voice was only
in my mind
and I killed
that certain part of me
that finally set
my soul free.

Sometimes, Like Now

Sometimes,
I feel that I am floating;
stuck someplace in-between
the heavens above and this planet's
gravitational pull. I can be at
any place at any time,
but I wasn't there when your time came;
turning below my feet, the world
goes on while I remain in this
fixated state, denial...

Sometimes,
I ask questions I know
cannot be answered because
I do not understand the reasons
behind the unknown. I have lost
so many and will lose so many more,
never will I be prepared enough;
continuing to breathe, moving on
while relishing memories,
selfish becomes me...

Sometimes,
I wish I could cry
to let out all the things
that have been building up inside.
Somewhere in the process, the tears
have all dried up as I became brittle;
cracks are all that remain
and the widening is what hurts,
so when I feel empty, I say...

Sometimes,
I wish I could disappear,

       like now...

just out of reach

as much as he says he doesn't, he loves attention - the more, the merrier. while trying to seem as standoffish as possible, more people seem to gravitate towards him, and when he is alone, all he wants is the company of others. he says he has too many friends, but continuously leaves an impression of his presence upon a majority of those who happen to cross his path. one could either look at that as if it were a scar, or that warm, tingly sensation that occupies every square inch of our being when we have those fluttery butterflies in our bellies.

a truly amazing entity, he is, as i have watched him over for many a year. riding through life like it was a hell-bent rollercoaster, tightly teetering back and forth on the edge of destruction; he is a beautiful mess. his intentions are as pure as a child's innocence, but his actions sometimes prove to be dramatically drastic. i have witnessed this vibrating soul do everything from saving lives in death's crosshairs, to stealing merchandise in order to support a drug habit. at this moment, he is swinging more

towards the righteous side of life, but he has
been on this path before.

i sometimes wonder if he will ever fully awaken.
the sleep he was born into has been slowly
washing away with every encounter to date, but
his stubbornness to grow up and stop acting
oblivious to his reckless nature has kept him
under a certain naivety that cannot be dismissed.
occasionally, i find myself wishing i could just
reach out and help to guide him toward the light,
or slap the living shit out of him, but we could
never come in any form of contact with each
other. you see, i am always somewhere in the
background, just out of reach, and all i can do is
sit back and watch his life unfold before the both
of us, for i am merely the reflection.

...to let go

whispers annihilate,
dance around,
spiraling,
weaving,
in and out,
fondling
this jaded mind.
dirty secrets,
dying
for another chance
to live
one more time,
flood the surface.
hearing the itch,
feeling the call
of the beast within;
obsessive predilection;
compulsive perversion.
eschew the feeding,
perpetuation.
overconfidence
proved insincere,
volition remains;
this is
not the end.

caught up just a little too far...

Nothing but an Outline

I had a dream last night that seemed so real, I almost believed that I was alive. Everything was in Technicolor, and there was no lag time whatsoever. Smooth-running graphics followed my every step through this magical, three-dimensional world of animation. Before long, I was flying through cyan-filled skies with jaden forests quickly passing below me. That was about the time that curiosity possessed my mind. I cannot be alone in this world of wonder, so who else was here before me to create such a magnificent place?

As soon as that question popped into my mind, my answer quickly knocked me to the ground; one hell of a blow to the back of the head, I might add. Skulls and bones began to circle my peripheral vision as I tried to shake it off. When I pulled myself up to my feet, I turned around to find my attacker.

There she stood, in all her glory; twice my size in height and mass, fully toned and equally upset. For a second, I thought I was in love, and then she lashed out again. Her nails were more like claws, razor sharp, with the uncanny ability to extend or detract at will. Time seemed to slow down at this moment, as I could see tracers following her movements, and not a second too soon; I quickly managed to jump backwards and out of her immediate reach.

She advanced on me again, spilling poison from her lips, like fire, in an unknown dialect. I could feel my pulse in my eardrums as she screamed her holy terror at me. What had I done to upset this being, and more importantly, how was I to defend myself from the wrath she was intent on lying upon me? Fear rapidly overwhelmed my senses, and I looked for anything to protect myself with.

I ran into the forest, looking for fallen branches, rocks or anything else I could use as a weapon. She had apparently been expecting this type of behavior, because there was nothing but lush, green grass overflowing amongst the trees. I think she was quite amused with my attempt at fleeing so quickly, as she only followed shortly behind for an even shorter amount of time. She was catching up with me and I still had nothing in the form of a defense tool. Anxiety-ridden, I began to panic; soon this game of cat and mouse was sure to be over.

I saw what appeared to be a clearing in the distance ahead. Unfortunately, once I moved past the trees, I found myself running into a brick wall, a dead end. No sooner had I turned around to find her breathing fumes of intense animosity all about me. The sky began to darken, and expansive electrical storms began to roll in. My survival instincts quickly flooded my train of thought again.

She threw her right arm out towards me in such a fluid motion, that it appeared she had cut the air between us. I ducked out of the way and tried to use her force against her. When I touched her reptilian skin, it burned my palms and smoke began to rise, so I had no choice but to let go of her. This was her approval of my demise; she began to laugh, and with the raise of her arms, in a cross-like figure, she spouted out a curse that made the wall begin to surround and envelop me.

Wasting no time, she sprang from the ground outside this prison, and then headed in my direction in full force. She grew in size and seemed to completely cover the opening that was above me a second earlier. Crystalline tears formed in my eyes, as trepidation dripped from their lids. Her forked tongue hissed towards me, making the wall shatter like brittle glass. Suddenly, her overgrown will to destroy penetrated everything that made me up.

A rainbow of colors began to bleed out from my open wounds. I was getting dizzy and noticed my body turning black and white. All that was shading my previous existence was quickly dripping around me. I collapsed into a pool of pigmentation, as my life drained about what was left of me, nothing more than an outline, a sketch, of someone that once was alive.

prayer to him

father, please forgive me,
for i have sinned;
i am following in the same footsteps
that you walked in.
even though i know the path
will only lead me to
the exact same place
that it finally took you;
which hurt me so very bad,
not to mention others,
causing me to close up inside,
so now it really bothers me...

me, who am i now that i am
"all grown up...?"
over a quarter of a century old
but still screwed up.
don't want to go a day without
some form of a drug;
hell, i can't even feel
the comfort of a hug,
much less the thought
of a head that is clear.
does this mean
that the end is near...?

so here i sit and write
as if i were talking to you
and you could verbally tell me
what it is that i should do;
which i know is something
that could never possibly happen
but i will still pray for it
even while i am dying.
though i am not quite ready
to leave here so soon,
so i have one last favor
to ask of you...

i wish that you would come
into a dream of mine,
show me what i should do
and how i should feel inside.
help me through
these times of confusion
because i am sure
you know the final conclusion,
to stop me from making
the same mistakes
and causing that many
more heartaches...

Brighten the Light

Feeling dirty,
a little uneasy;
dying to scratch an itch
that is just out of reach.
And the meantime
is filled with anxiety;
what can I do
to forget all of this?

The future is so
unpredictable,
and the past belongs
far behind us,
but nightmares chase
every waking thought,
and I'm losing my mind
with every passing moment.

This perverted desire
still lies dormant
somewhere in the
depths of my mind.

The day is bright
as the night is dark,

and dusk is lost
somewhere in between,
and the rain never washed
this oily residue away;
only lifted it up
as it rose to the top.

So, I slip and I slide,
careful not to fall,
grabbing anything
to hold me fast,
but these hands are worn
and torn with time;
this running has me
so ready to rest.

Looking upwards,
a sigh escapes these lungs
and forgiveness is begged
of a crime not yet committed,
as the ritual begins
to slowly decay
every ethical thought
that penetrated this lapse.

It is never enough.

Immensity

Pain, it seems, shall sometimes never leave
and muscle memory is all that remains.
The past sticks with us in so many ways,
and as we forgive, we cannot ever forget
the reasons behind those scarring events.
Love has come, and it has gone; essentially
those times are forever lost in a void
of confusion, depression and despair.
The weight of it all pulls me under,
sinking to new depths of doubt and fear.

The light strobes, cutting and sinking
into the darkness of this blinding limbo.
What was there is now gone, as tracers
follow the steps of us walking away. By
and by, we continue to try to tread waters
which contain depths we shall never know.
Out of breath and energy, we shall sink
to the levels which touched Atlantis.
Life jackets are supposed to preserve
the ability to stay afloat, but stronger
currents have more in mind these days.

The red sea is sucking the life out of me,
as the black sea consumes my security.

Waters run deep, and cleanse the soul,
but these lungs are filling up too quickly.
Every breath contains gurgles of hope
lost between bubbles of uncertainty.
Giving in, just to let go, is too easy,
and the sinking feels way too natural.
This wavy world, underneath currents of life,
tempts my soul to drift away to coral
and plankton, fish food and moving silt.

it never fails

ominous thoughts
cloud the mind
every time street lights go out
as they are being passed,
for it is a sign,
but who can read the language?

every path before me
has been overrun
with nothing but black cats,
thirteen of them
to be exact,
every
single
time.

it all adds up,
eventually,
every receipt
has a balance of $6.66,
no matter what is picked up -
the calling.

stepped outside today,
the stench of death

all around us:
me,
you,
everyone.

looking up
towards the light in the sky
for answers,
just another street light,
burning out,
as it is being passed.

as virgin as it gets

with broken and bare feet, i tread along a thorn
filled path, unsure of my final destination, with
only one direction in mind. to my left are dark,
desolate valleys, and to my right, the high hills
and mountains reach up to touch the cloudy sky.
i move forward in search of new light, for i leave
behind me the ominous storms which have led
me to this point.

in the not too far-off distance, i can hear the
soothing sounds of running water, winding their
way through rocky land, beckoning me, drawing
me closer. i step into a dense forest, surrounding
myself deeper within the emerald overgrowth,
seeking the babbling brook, which is calling my
name. darkness engulfs me, yet again, as i push
onward, between the trees, but fear no longer
has a place inside this sacred heart of mine.

as fallen branches and twigs crackle under the
weight of my movement, many smaller animals
scurry away, hurriedly, to find shelter. an owl,
safe inside the decaying hole of a tree, watches
me closely as i move past him. a serpent hisses
as he slithers his way through a patch of wild

ivy, which spreads itself around the trunk of a
fern; knowing all of this makes me realize that
we are never as alone as we would sometimes
like to believe.

soon i enter a new clearing and my treasured
waters run swiftly ahead of me. as i walk up and
along the shore, the moving currents cause an
intoxicating mist to rise through the air, in which
i breathe, and immediately my senses are
overwhelmed with a hypnotizing effect. i step
into the vast pool, unafraid, to cleanse myself of
any and all impurities; it is much cooler than
expected and immediately a heightened state of
awareness is awakened within me.

already, my ability to feel has become much
more sensitive. ripples in the water are coming
to me in threes and every grain of sand between
my toes can be accounted for. the sound of silt
moving back and forth from the undertow,
caused by the rising of the waves in the distance,
is almost deafening. i must continue forward.

as i reach new depths, i can smell that which was
no longer innocent burning behind me, as the
heat quickens my pulse. my peripheral line of
sight has completely surrounded me, and the
flames that are licking the sky are burning in

vivid colors of blue, green and purple. i begin to tread these waters that recreate my presence and can taste the ashes that were my old self, for i am being reborn, omnisciently.

weightlessly floating in the center of this liquid mass, i tilt my head upwards, as the heavens begin to sing. a bright flash appears above me and an unknown force drags me below the translucent surface. purging deeper into my waters, the light moves further away from me, and i enter an asphyxiated state of unconsciousness.

upon reawakening, i realize that i have reached a new higher ground. all uncertainty and fear, which plagued my previous existence, dissipated into my shadows, and i shall now move forward without ever looking back.

the end, or is it the beginning...?

serenity

the memories i still have inside burn almost
every single hole
that fill up my tainted self and my contaminated
soul
with broken promises, regrets, dreams that never
did come true
the past, it holds so many things; the future will
hold many too
so look ahead and not behind, the future is more
important
nothing could possibly matter if it is not
significant
to the things that are to come and everything that
will soon be
leave the past where it belongs and you will find
serenity.

Unreality

I had a dream
that was so beautiful,
I awoke with tears
in my eyes
because it was not
a reality...

distant

saw your face today
in a picture, on a screen,
so beautiful and delicate,
completely inspiring.
sunshine kissed your cheeks;
wind animated your hair;
flowers grew after every step;
footprints of you being there.
some birds began to sing
in a tree just out of sight;
butterflies and ladybugs
around you, they took flight.
every substance came to life
by being graced with you;
about that time, i got sad
because i couldn't be there too.

porcelaneous

skin,
like porcelain,
frail,
translucent ceramic,
brittle
yet reflective;
i see myself...

smooth
and pure,
abusive
towards glass,
shatters,
spider-web effect,
remaining unharmed...

cold,
to the touch,
3rd degree
freezer-burn,
jumps
at the thought,
only to return...

beauty,

dancing in the light,
shadows
shall never know,
darkness
will never see;
it is still there...

leaks
whenever cracked,
puddle,
full of regrets,
broken
beyond repair,
only to be replaced...

Boiling Point

I am the water in the pot, on your stove, over the open flame, which you continuously watch, impatiently waiting for the moment that this synthesis reaches the boiling point. Millions of miniscule molecules racing around and into each other at a rate of speed so fast, your eyes wouldn't have the slightest chance of keeping up. Still you continue to stare in that condescending manner that you pride yourself with, pouring more salt into the open wound, as if that will help.

The steam continues to rise, and though I may be timid, I am just as livid, and the longer you gawk, the more intense my fervor becomes to give into the dark desire of burning you. I might just relinquish what you so desperately seek if you would only take this admonishment to heart and look elsewhere, because the scrutiny is presumptuous, trite and discouraging.

Alliteratious

As always, I am all alone
because of my belligerent behavior,
casually, yet cautiously, ceasing creation
due to my deadening, dormant decisions,
effectively eradicating any expectations
from my fragile, fatigued mind.
Grasping for life, I grunt and groan, praying for
help, my head is my home, and my heart
is insecure from inviting these invading
jokers inside; the juxtaposition just
kills me. I'm the kind that wants a keeper.
Though
lonely, I live to love, one that lasts
more than a minute, not merely a moment. A
new nerve says it's now or never; I must be
open and optimistic or this oppression will
prove to be the pit of my pitiful existence and
queue the queen of heart's best quality, to
retrieve my head, and I really want to relieve
some of the stress that's been stored up for so
long, but
the truth of the matter is that there is
ultimately an underlying understanding
underneath this
very vast void – I must get over my fear.

With whom, what, when where and how to do
this, I must
exemplify my examples of exactly what can
happen. I
yearn for you, my youthful lover, for this
zero is zip until we reach zen together.

Jahya

I remember the day she whispered her name into the cold January winter morning air, and her breath seemed to linger in the atmosphere for an eternity. I swear I can still hear that sweet tone, massaging my eardrums and inner lobes. Some sounds just have this intoxicating resonance to them, as do certain individuals.

Her alabaster skin glimmered under the soft, pale moonlight, and her cerulean eyes sparkled like flawless diamonds under fluorescent inspection. The smile that escaped through the space between her lips had such purity in it that incurable diseases suddenly seemed to have some form of hope. She also had this colorful glowing aura that seemed to envelop her at times, and I guess that is why I didn't really notice that she never touched the ground; she was always floating about three inches above the surface of this planet, which has us slaved down to it.

'Jahya' is the tender vibration that slipped out of her mouth and mingled with fascination in the back of my mind. Even though I couldn't remember ever hearing that name before, it was very reminiscent of what I remembered home to be, which is strange because I have been an orphan as long as I can recall, and never really had a steady home. Nonetheless, I was thrown into a state of delirium once those soothing syllables penetrated my audible range of perception.

From that moment on, I have been in a constant blackout state, and only certain pieces of my memory have been attainable at this point. I slightly remember what seemed to resemble the shape of wings behind her, but they were much darker than her shimmering self, as if they were in the shadows, hidden. I also recall the growing caliginosity, as if the sun was going down for its final time. The sunset in those short moments reminded me of what the blind were missing; the majestic colors of amber, tangerine and crimson seemed to entwine themselves with amethyst and indigo, creating a breath-taking display of chromaticity.

I am suddenly reminded of my constriction of breath, and everything beginning to slowly fade away, into this crepuscular position, below that levitating entity. I am surrounded by shadows, and through the obscurity, I can see something

draw near. It is that angelic face, only there has
been some form of distorted interference
between us. I can see her ensanguined lips curl,
as a lustrous flash cover them, similar to the
fashion of an index finger. This is about the time
I always enter a syncopic capacity. I'm trying to
talk, but I can't. I want to ask if that is a blade
shining in the darkness, but all I hear is that
beautiful voice again, 'shhh...'

For the All in Us

Could you please help us turn the "m" in me
Upside-down, creating the "w" in We;
Effectively smashing this egotistic enemy,
Bringing into light some form of tranquility
We've been pining for in life?
For, it has now been revealed that We
Are all holding onto very similar keys
To everything in life, including insecurities,
Suffering, strife and also the abilities
To change all that's wrong to right.
So, let us begin by changing our ways,
Starting with our thoughts and all we say,
Therefore, turning over every night into day,
Creating this spark of light that just may
Conquer this draining darkness.
With promises of an everlasting love
Showering upon us from the heavens above,
Warming up our souls, like a hand inside a
glove;
Attaining the peace and serenity of a dove
Flying high above the abyss.

Cooling Blood

Have you ever felt the warm, sticky feeling of another person's life force dripping down any portion of your body, if not multiple, leaving behind crimson trails of justified coagulation? Did you happen to notice the cooling effect during that process, or were you so smitten with the mission's completion that important, little details, such as those, were the furthest forms of contemplation from your immediately necessary attention? Maybe it was just all too much going on in such a short amount of time that the shock took over and you really do have no recollection of any events at all, or perhaps these episodes did not even really take place to begin with. What in the hell have you done; where in God's name have you been; when has this ever been acceptable and how are you going to justify the pathetic attempts at some form of a viable excuse for explaining the reasons why they were allowed to take place to begin with?

Opalescent Purity

Blue would be the color
that forms before my eyes
every time the thought of you
crosses over my mind,
because it has been ages
since I have seen your face
and my intense desire
fills up this empty space,
to the point this lonely tone
slowly begins to fade
from its melancholy hue
into an iridescent shade;
the way fire looks through ice
opalescent purity:
purple, red, yellow, orange,
milky white and green.
And I will close my eyes
so, I can fall asleep,
just so I can dream of you,
a dream I'll always keep,
because you are the light
that brightens up my life,
and the one whom I send love
when I say my prayers at night.

Contrite Consternation

Confusion consumes the footprints
left in the sands of this ever-changing
journey through heaven and hell.
Opportunities present themselves,
and effects happen to follow as well.
Decisions are hard to make when
multiple choices add up, and time
is always against every open moment.

Happiness should be permanent, but
it comes and goes like rain. Some days
it pours, and others, it never arrives.
Good company is wet times, and boredom
is drought. The endless search can be
very overwhelming at times, and proves
to be pointless, mostly. Maybe giving up
is the key to it finding those in need.

Melancholy moments may be few and
far between, but they carry a heavy weight
that has this residual effect in dark corners.
Shadows play games with candlelight, while
voices whisper things that should never
be told. Idle intervals only add to this madness,
and the insanity can be quite destructive;
it is good to always stay as busy as possible.

Demons are screaming in this direction, and
their audible range is impossible to ignore.
Excuses are only reasons something was
failed, and they seem to prevail these days;
justifications are just another bad seed,
helping these weeds to reach new heights. It's
been raining lately, but the precipitation seems
to be more like the perspiration of weariness.

Strength can be built up over these periods,
but fatigue promotes atrophy, and these
parched pauses tend to lead to lethargic
destinations. The blinding light has been
eclipsed again, and this duration is devastating.

Gods may be watching over, but their tongues
could be very useful in times like these; this
waxy buildup needs to be cleared away,
deliberately.

Translucent Opacity

Once upon a peachy day,
holiday, not much to do;
observing as my candle burned,
reminded yours truly of you.

Tapered edge gently unwrapped,
rendezvous, definite must;
ignited the virgin wick,
reminiscent of pure lust.

Desire's alter, burning fire,
flickered yet another way;
wax liquefied, dripped about,
devoted atheist's hands prayed.

Vividly the vibrant flame
ignited intentionally;
melted dreams covered a bottle,
translucent opacity.

Molding rounded polished edges,
marvelously flawed, not fake;
candelabra centerpiece
divinely fated, shalt not break.

What burned away lethargically
manifested, became truth;
manufactured bountifully,
impeccably, same as you.

Eternity's Ripple

First time our eyes ever crossed
Felt you deep inside my soul
Past and present, many times
Morphed relations, fate controlled
Contracts signed and sealed by atman
Lessons to learn this time around
Our true spirits, bodies, minds
In this school, on this playground
We dance and sing and laugh and play
Bound by this blood, this flesh, this bone
The highest lands, the deepest oceans
Every grain of sand and stone
Of all that is and what shall be
This karmic cycle circles 'round
Bounding us to one another
Separate footing, different ground
While synchronicities add up
We are all one in the same
Simultaneous harmonies
True creator's board and game
Of chess and skill, ultimate fate
Transcendence from this physical
State of consciousness, now pondered,
Should not be questioned, this is real
For we are simply entities

Spiritual beings thus having
Human plagued experiences
In this other dimension
This me shall wait and ponder all
This life's possibilities
Manifest eternal love
And bathe in the reality.

Lifeless Satellite

Silently drifting along
within this cosmos,
bound by one thing,
attraction, drawn together;
slowly rotating onward,
instinctive, yet manipulative.
Heavenly bodies exist,
form mass and simply are,
as moons orbit planets,
planets orbit stars;
following celestial paths
mapped out in numbers,
beyond comprehension,
lies all of the answers.

as a guiding light,
sun, you are
gravitational pivot,
perfectly centered,
constantly pulling inward,
never pushing away,
infinitely drawing closer,
mother-like, in a loving way,
sharing, caring, nurturing life,
existence is co-dependent.

super-nova cataclysm,
satellite floats, lost in space,
quietly set adrift, isolated
inside this vast universe,
searching for signals, awaiting
intermittent transmission-
something, anything, nothing;
lights slowly fade, burn out
in time, everything dies
alone…

Enchanted

I walked outside today and gazed among the dusty hue that covers up this concrete jungle known of as Dallas, and as I tried to see past the high-rise nightline, I realize that I am a slave to this place. I admit that I want to leave but for some reason, I'm afraid to go. I guess that there are just people here that I don't want to leave behind, which I know that I would never let something like that go on forever, but right now I really just don't want to have to even try.

I feel like I am stuck inside a giant spider web, frantically trying to get away, but I'm attached by the threads that somehow hold this broken town together with one string that intertwines itself with every single fucking thing that our society looks over, but we all know to be corrupt; too many are afraid to tell us who they really trust. So, they will each perish, confused and all alone, inside of what they claim to be their humble home which has a leaking ceiling and a cracked foundation; things get so much worse when there is no motivation, and that is where I feel most of us try to hide, emotional boundaries that lie within mental genocide.

I sincerely wish people would take a step back and look from a different point of view; they could see that we are all the same and only our ideas would be new, though it may be too much to ask of a world, tired of itself, when so many others are just hurting someone else, but if they could only stop taking everything for granted, then maybe life would feel just a little more enchanted...

Contradiction

The only time
I feel lonely
is whenever I think
I need somebody
to fill up the holes in my life.

But those will come
and hoes will go,
the same way that life
passes us by,
and in the end
it is all the same,
though we may never know
the reasons why.

We all want some things,
there are others that we need,
but somewhere in the process
we get caught up in greed,
so we will always get
whatever we deserve,
and we will always know
when we are pinching on those nerves.

But who can stop us

when we are all guilty,
especially whenever
we all want to be free?
Which is the complete opposite
of everything I have said,
but if I told you the truth,
you would believe a lie instead.

The Truth That Hurts

Why does it have to hurt so bad,
wanting something you will never have?
The one real wish that never came true
will definitely come back to you,
making you really wonder why
you put out the effort to try.
Still, you block out voices in your head,
"I swear I'll try until I'm dead",
but empty promises prevail,
dragging you through the depths of hell,
while the secret sound of silent screams
makes you hold on to all of your dreams.

Still, you try to win the race,
filled up with only disgrace,
while ugliness covers inside;
slowly, your emotions have died.
Until you feel you're all alone,
"I am so ready to go home,
but I know no one is waiting for me;"
is this how you feel when you are free?
Walking away with empty hands,
blood-stained tears and ignored demands
until you reach the bitter end,
figuring out who are real friends.

Now, you know you're not all by yourself,
but you cannot blame anyone else,
when it was you who planted the seeds
of all your wants and all your needs.

Waiting for that Change

I've had a lot on my mind lately,
mainly to do with the world;
knowing what's right or wrong
while feeling alone and cold.

We're living in this concrete jungle
that we all try to call life;
I know it will be cut off soon
with a very rusted, dull knife.

I'm just waiting for a chance
for it to all start over again…

Heard many stories about it,
have a few of my own;
it is all about the master plan,
which is something I have known.

Nothing lasts forever,
everything must come to an end;
I feel like the time is here,
I want it to begin.

I'm just waiting for a chance
for it to all start over again;
I'm waiting for that change
that will take away this sin…

I'm tired of this corruption,
people's lack of control;
I'm tired of our government
that keeps digging this hole;
I'm tired of society,
putting others on a shelf;
I'm tired of this world,
and I think it's tired of itself.

But I'm not going to worry,
it will all be fixed soon.
I am just going to wait
because we're already doomed,
and I can honestly say
I don't mind wearing this frown,
because I'm looking forward
to watching it all fall down.

So, when the shit hits the fan,
I don't want to see you cry;
we all know that it is destiny
for everyone to die.

Just do yourself a favor,
climb out of your hidey-hole,
and you just might have a chance
to save what's left of your soul.

Thorn in the Flesh

Desire,
the lonesome touch
that leaves you begging for more.

Longing,
the idle time
that passes as you slowly burn.

Yearning,
the black bile
that fills up this dejection.

Salacity,
the impurity within
that fuels the hunger of this infatuation.

Depression,
the only comfort
that remains, for it will always be there.

Malignity,
the final straw,
breaking the camel's back, causing him to fall.

Endless Maze

Heard that loneliness is just a phase
when in fact it is an endless maze;
an emotional boundary on which you live
with nothing else left to give.
Still, you try to succeed,
while love is all you really need,
but you hold on to all your fears,
broken hearts and endless tears.

So, you are left all by yourself
with no one to blame but yourself.
Now emptiness fills up inside;
running out of places to try and hide.
All alone, you fade away,
hoping to try another day,
but why bother when no one cares;
none of this will ever seem fair.

It does not work or is not right,
sleep all day, stay up all night;
banging your head against the wall,
waiting for someone to catch you fall
until you hit the bottom and finally see
that everybody gets lonely.

Birthday Presents

Ahh, nothing like those good ol' parent-to-child pep talks. They really seem to motivate children these days; you got the do's, the don'ts, the rights and the wrongs, and all we ever wanted to know was why. It's a little strange how people naturally tend to look upward whenever that question is raised.

One year, on my birthday, my mother and I had one of those important conversations:

"Ok, I've given you all of your birthday presents, now where are mine?"

[chuckles] "You don't get any presents; it's my birthday, not yours."

"Well, I feel that the parents, or at least mothers, should get presents on their children's birthdays."

"And why is that?"

Tilting her head toward the texturized ceiling, she replies, "simply because mothers have to carry their children around, in their bellies, for nine months before having them ripped out. On this very day, thirteen years ago, I was at the hospital, in excruciating pain, for many hours, just trying to birth you. You would be absolutely amazed to see what a woman goes through during childbirth."

"I have seen it in health class, and it was pretty gross."

"You might think it's gross now, but I can promise you it is one of the most amazing things that will ever happen to any parent... well, next to having grandchildren."

"I'm not having kids, sorry."

"Well, I did, and it's your birthday, so I want a present, for being your mother."

Being the sly, smartass that I am, I eyeballed my brand new skateboard in the corner, by the front door, and looked up to her, smiling, while saying, "ok, since you went through so much pain to bring me into this world, and since you are a cool mother, I am going to give you a full day of peace and quiet, because I am out of here!"

No sooner did those words escape my mouth,
and a wooden door was slamming shut behind
me. She chased after me, but I was already
heading down the street, and she yelled out,
"remember, I brought you into this world; I can
just as easily take you out of it."

Just imagine what the neighbors thought.

No Exclusions

Life
Offers
Various
Emotions,

Although none of them could ever be
of more importance than the simple
act of love; as tough as it may appear
at times, love is simply everything.

Some say it is better to have and lose
than to never have at all; that the bitterness
makes greater the sweetness, however
the meantime can experience painful throes.

We all need love, so it is imperative
to remember to not only radiate beautiful
energy, but also learn to accept all positivity
into our lives as well: infinite exchanges…

Learning
Opens
Vile
Eyes,

Always
Live
Love...!

Y?

Let my first love slip away by my own
insecurity,
time passed slowly by; never knew just what to
say.
Held these feelings in for just a bit too long,
now knots are being tied and I'm not feeling too
strong.

Had this picture-perfect world set inside my
mind,
but it is slowly decaying to be left far behind.
Can't handle this feeling, with no place to go;
trying to deal with it properly, even though I am
alone.

You are the one on my mind; you are the one in
my heart;
you are everything I feel, now I am torn apart.
So, as you see me behind you in everything that
you do,
I guess that I will swallow my heart and every
single thing else too.

Terminally Eminent

I feel as if I am stuck in a terminally downward spiral, feet above the head and without a parachute to unravel, aggressively gaining speed and velocity as the seconds quickly begin stretching inches into miles. Has your life ever flashed before your eyes, giving you some sense of purpose afterwards? Well, this flashing won't stop, and an epileptic seizure appears to be on the eminent horizon, but how soon and for how long before the final splat of this super active set of vibrations screech to a completely dead halt?

Enlightenment

Remember when it all began?

That gentle age where not much mattered, something to do at the time. You know, it all seemed so cool; we were the young and almighty, invincible to the world. Nothing could possibly beat us down, these strong and willful souls.

Heavens watch from above as devils prey down below; the ignorance of innocence, the fuel that feeds the fire. Naivety played an important role in the downfall of morality, more of a reason to let it all go; an excuse for a justification.

The grip was slowly lost, it had a slippery feel anyways; a snowball progression of sorts, straight to the bottom of it all. Flat on the ground, in a pinned-down state, sinking from forces below; wallowing in self-pity while drowning in confusion.

A light suddenly appears, inviting but also
blinding; we only see what we want anyways,
so, sight is selective; open yourself up, free the
mind of everything and let forces unknown to
man try to make a residual effect.

To knock down all the walls, destroy the
complete ego, free the spirit and the mind;
letting the knowledge seep inside to the point
that we can grow, feel free to be inspired, take
comfort in this world and become the things we
once aspired to be.

Burning the Bush

You make me smell
the roses when
otherwise, I
would be burning
the bush.

Restless Soul

What the hell am I supposed to do
to make this pathetic fucking excuse
of a reality understand that no matter
what you do, you cannot change my
inner spirit. You can lock me up and
throw away the key, put a bullet
through my membranes, skin me alive
or lead me to the guillotine, and I will
smile the whole time, because my soul
is screaming to be released of these shackles
and chains that hold me to this materialistic
black hole of humanity. Please make my
fucking day by splitting this flesh and
bone apart, so I can finally escape,
because I cannot free myself and
I am sick of waiting for you to do it.

in the works

i have this pain inside me,
you are so beautiful;
taste just like eye candy,
feel you in my soul.
there is a piece that's missing
somewhere in between;
you look like you would fit me,
so clean and so serene...

to become whole
is to be one...

i have been hiding this side
get scared and run away;
it hurt so bad the first time,
don't want to feel that way.
there is a cycle started,
it is almost complete,
once it has been broken,
i'll finally be free...

to become whole
is to be one,
one and only one...

no more running away,
or hiding from the truth;
there is nothing to fear,
i have nothing left to prove,
i am being reborn,
breaking out of my shell,
this is a new beginning;
my soul can finally heal...

hit me again

i drink alone, in solitude,
while no one else is around
to release my emotions
built up just to tear me down;
letting go of those feelings,
thoughts i held so very dear,
getting past insecurities
swallowing all of my tears...

but numbness is a crutch
used as an excuse
to justify mistakes
that are known as abuse...

i know that i live a lie
and realize i am not true;
do not follow my shadow
or you will end up turning blue
like bodies rotting in a morgue,
meat hung in the slaughterhouse,
it does not ever stop right here,
it only gets so much worse…

like lying to your family
or stealing from your friends,

maybe cheating on your girl
because it all does depend...

on whether you have the strength
or muster up the willpower
to put poisonous bottles down
instead of asking for another,
but it is far too easy
having that last, final drink;
drowning yourself in sorrow
among other vile things…

inside the mind

inside the mind of a junkie and not sure what he
will do next;
thoughts that revolve in his mind do not make
much sense;
all that matters is the high he will soon receive
doing anything to get cash; it is so deceiving.

all he wants is to feel a good high,
and he's willing to take that chance
when he knows that he can die.

crazy thoughts run through his head, confusion
is his mental block,
heroin is his medicine, withdrawal would be his
thought,
but needles are his problem, so his tracks won't
go away;
all he does is justify, telling himself that it's
okay.

all he wants is to feel a good high,
and he's willing to take that chance
when he knows that he can die.

open your eyes and look at the light, it will show
you what's wrong or right,
but he'll break apart his healing sticks just so he
can get another fix.
he does not want his high to end because he
thinks it is his only friend;
in reality, nothing more than lies; camouflaged
truth in euphoric disguise.

he will continue his trip until he can realize
that he does not need it, or until he dies,
but he will not stop for anyone else
when he won't even do it himself.

read the end today

read the end today...

not as beautiful
as the story
would have led you
to believe.

cliffhanger...

wide the fuck open
to let the mind run wild;
wondering what to expect
while wanting it to be over.

something feels unfinished...

reminiscent aftertaste
of something
that never made it past
the tip of the tongue.

reflections of the past...

a silhouette
chasing a shadow,

trying to outrun
the footprints left behind.

the mirror never lies...

the tight grip,
bloodshot eyes,
fixed and dilated,
gasping for reason,
asphyxia.

the light,
the dark,
the touch,
the burn,
the blood,
the pain,
the scars,
and of course the fingerprints.

heard you say it was over
and for the life of me,
cannot recall
when anything really ever began...

Breadth

Two peculiar existences,
consecrated divinities,
lie years away
from each other
in a world that is
way too small
for them to be
so far apart. One
is dying to live
as the other
lives to die. Both
mind blue ardors
while fondling caliginosity.
and as they bourgeon
in the great depression, they
writhe from the deliberation
that they could ever
feel so alone, as they
share the same moon.

inadequate

85

i am a broken record,
a needle scratch,
a skip in your life…

i am a rusty halo,
a broken promise,
a dirty deed…

i want to be a part,
a single piece,
some significance…

i need an excuse,
a lot of attention,
some form of reason…

you are so perfect,
you have everything,
you need nothing…

and i am here
missing pieces,
inadequate...

Lockdown

The weight of it all
rests heavily on this soul,
and that burden alone
is beginning to wear me thin,
for the static in the walls
is screaming out my name,
while the face of time points,
laughingly in this direction,
and all that can be done
is to keep lifting this chin
every single time
they try to pull it down again.
But I have grown weary
of all the childish games
that are played on this mind
during their manipulation,
so, I will look ahead,
as I refuse to look away,
taking all the lashings
they are willing to hand out,
because my day will soon come
to be released of these chains,
and the walls will start to bleed
once I regain my name.

little did i know

i'm still dealing with feelings
i thought were in the past;
little did i know these things
were something that would last
until the day would finally come
i would simply cease to be,
but that time has not come yet;
it is still deep within me.

so here i sit all by myself
without much left to do,
thoughts revolve around my head,
all of which are about you;
wondering which way this life,
or what we call it will end up being,
when i cannot forget my past,
or any of my formal feelings.

whenever nothing makes sense,
simply because it is not right;
i really do not want to deal
with any of this torment tonight,
because it is the frustration
that i cannot understand,
all the pain and lost emotion
that i have been dealt firsthand.

whenever i had to give up
everything i thought was true;
now I am stuck inside this place,
cold and lonely without you.
whenever i did truly think
this was now all in the past,
little did i know these things
would somehow fucking last…

Reminder

I've lost the ability in myself to control the
anger,
for I am mad, extremely pissed, at the lack of
respect;
wanting, expecting and bitching a little more
makes it hard to relax and even to exhale.

And I do not want to feel that way,
don't wish to thrive on stale behavior,
I will not lower myself and stoop to that level;
I must learn to breathe deeper.

In my waking, in the serene state, I'm perfectly
comfortable,
and then you push, begin to shove, strangling
my patience,
killing my will to want and to try to understand
the reasons behind those selfish actions.

Is this a lesson yet to be learned?
And who is the teacher?
In through the nose and out through the mouth;
I must learn to breathe deeper.

broken cycle

in the early hours past midnight,
while most of the world is asleep,
i sit up all alone thinking
about the things that i have done;
i'm sure that everyone
has been lost or confused,
but how many of them
did what i have become...?

pleasure and pain go hand in hand,
too much of one can kill the other,
so i squeezed the trigger to forget it all;
problem solved? no, just another…

until i begin to fade away;
what was i worried about anyway?

feelings i don't remember having
slip my mind once again
maybe they'll return to me,
maybe just the same old sin
if not tomorrow, another day
it always seems to depend
but how can it ever stop,
when it doesn't want to end...

Descent

Closing the shades
that cover the soul
windows, giving into
the melancholy sounds and
what lies behind them, legs
crossed, sitting upright,
head tilted back,
silently spinning
right, without moving
an inch, entering the descent,
the downward spiral
to new depths of a pit
that is bottomless.

irritation

i have an itch i cannot scratch,
it is under my skin,
and now that it is dead
it has started peeling;
it is showing me sides
of sensitivity
and it is driving me mad,
oh god, please help me...

it started as an irritation
that i tried to look past
and has turned into a nightmare
way too fucking fast;
the time has now come
to change a thing or two
so i can try to relieve myself
of the shit i'm going through...

but where do i start
when i am not sure where it will end?
well i guess that is up to you,
#1 my friend...

hit me once again

the upper hand, such a prized
possession, take and give at will,
making decisions for the whole
of this community, like help
was asked of what is considered
inappropriate or wrong, we only
do this out of love, dedication;
inspiration comes in many forms,
abuse obviously comes in so many
more, like stopping something before
it has a chance to begin. greed is one
of the seven deadly sins and this squander
proves that power in the wrong hands
is nothing but a loss to us as a whole...

Removal

"Jack, it actually hurts; no sign of anything made
me feel better. I continually told her how I didn't
want it to change our relations, at least to the
worst, and she told me the same, but I find a
cold silence between us now. I was only honest,
like you told me to be, and NOW WHAT...?"

Don't listen to Jack, or Jill, or Jimmy, or your
fucking self anymore. I only wanted to believe
in the fairytale of something like love; now I'm
dealing with the lowest dregs of life. Don't listen
to your pain.

I'm quite indifferent at the moment. I was
honest, and all I received was abstractedness. It
wasn't a complete shove away as much as it was
a healthy push in that faithful direction. Either
way you want to look at it, sometimes more
harm is done rather than good.

"At least I'm no longer holding it all in...? How
could you arrive to this conclusion, unless it was
your plan all along? Yes, I'll agree that the
restraining of tightly woven emotions can be
trying on anyone, but do you not think the

unraveling spells pain out in another language?
My fucking God, the thought of killing myself,
just to rid you of my mind, is sounding more and
more pleasant every single second."

Ha-ha, that should shut him up for a few; I swear
sometimes I cannot get any time to myself. Wait
a minute, maybe I have too much time to myself
and he is my savior, my martyr and my crucified
sins in all their blacks and whites. Or maybe he
is the reason, alone, for all of this madness.

There is a knocking at the corner of my mind,
and I continue to sit here contemplating on
whether or not to acknowledge it. I realize it's
Jack, in all his vain attempts, to return in my
moment of shallow crawling, but I think I'll let
him scratch the windowpanes for a while. There
is something about a neurotic's mind that
shouldn't be fucked with at all, for it could very
quickly turn into a psychotic nightmare, and
that, my friends, would be trouble for everyone
in the near vicinity.

*Come out to play; it might be raining, but
you're dehydrated anyway, and in need of a
good purging. As I sit, the waters rise; at the
wave of my hand, they will dissipate. I create

this mist for you, and all of your clouded
thoughts, for the clearing is the most fun...*

Strange how one can make the loudest of noises,
while the stereo cannot gain a higher volume,
and still sounds have the ability to creep into the
backdoor of your mind. My mental deadlock has
broken Jack's ability to connive his way around
my head at the moment. One would have to
guess that a perfect silence has its evils as well.

There was a loud, crashing sound of glass and
steel in the background, yet I remained
unmoved. Whatever it is can come to me, for I
had better be its purpose! I only want to sit and
give you the honest truth, that I gave in to all my
inhibitions and they didn't do me much good. I
completely caved in and gave up a part of
myself that was held so dear, and it wasn't really
taken; I handed it out, but there it sat. I can hear
the footsteps now.

"I see you have brought chains; let me guess, the
better to hold me near? And duct tape, to silence
all those lonely screams that escaped as you
broke in. You are truly fass bucking ackwards,
my compadre. In case you haven't noticed, I no
longer care. I see you looking at me with
corruptive anger, and I cannot help but laugh.

Am I supposed to scream as you draw so near?
GIVE IT THE FUCK UP. I TRIED YOUR
UNWORTHY METHODS AND ALL IT DID
FOR ME WAS NOTHING!"

"Please don't let my complacency distract your
intentional motives; I deserve the full effect! The
chains that bound me to this thorn-covered
throne have rusted in your name. The duct tape
that bounds together my lips... (has faulty
adhesive, for my thoughts still roam. The
evaporation of gasoline on one's skin has a very
drying effect; this cannot be good for my vanity.
And what is the purpose of this ziplock bag over
my head; I would hope that you realize it's not
going to be yellow and blue makes green
moment!)"

The sulfur-smelling strike of a match,
intertwined with the cosmic glow of its spark, is
quite funny at the moment. See, I cannot smell,
due to the plastic bag over my head, and my
vision is blurred, for the same reason, but it is all
so very clear. I hope my smile shines through in
this moment that my life has pinnacled, for it is
now that all should take notice of the fact that I
gave in to the pleasures of everyone but myself,
and I am now being persecuted.

Isn't it strange how the heat from a fire can suck
the oxygen out of...

Ode to Beer

Beer is good,
beer is great,
I've been drinking beer
since about 8:00, and
even though I am not sober,
I do not feel a buzz;
I know this sounds confusing,
but I know it is because
alcohol's effect
on top of the brain
institutes belligerence,
which would be insane,
but after a few brews,
I don't seem to care;
whatever was bothering me
is no longer there,
until I wake up
the next morning
and realize I did
some stupid, fucked up thing
that no one will forget,
but I will never remember;
"oh my god,
what the hell did I say to her?"

So who do I ask
about the things I have done;
did I let myself turn into
what I did not want to become,
which would be a drunk,
or a pathetic fool;
did I turn one of my favorite toys
into a lethal tool
just to forget about
any painful thoughts
that my mind can embrace
or until my brain rots?
Kind of like my liver,
which is hard as a rock,
but filled up with holes,
exactly like my socks,
which should warm my feet,
on which I try to walk;
not only can't I do this,
but I cannot really talk,
much less read the sign that says,
"if you're drunk, you will not be tattooed",
but I just like beer because
beer is good food…

Red Angus

Looking at your face,
staring into your eyes,
wondering where you might be;
for there is emptiness
within great space;
I wonder if you can even see me.

Through all of the haze,
the blurry and fuzzy
moments we have shared together;
inside of this state,
locked in this trance,
and all I know is that I don't want to be here.

It is just too much for me,
more than I will handle,
I will not live down inside a hole
where I cannot breathe
and I cannot move;
I must remember to consider my soul.

I have been there before,
was there for too long,
and swore that I would not spend another day;
so I have let you go,

you are free to fly,
and knowing this, you will probably stay...

Luminosity

Feeling cold,
yet not quite numb,
these aching and icy,
tingling sensations
seem to span a lifetime
across this sense of self.
Pushing ever onward
through the iniquity,
in search of light,
and though I stumble,
I continue progressing.
The surrounding walls are
reminiscent of tombstones,
with words inscribed
speaking of brighter times.
Stepping forward, to leave
the cold, hollow darkness,
continuing to grow,
reaching luminescence,
wrapping itself around me,
bringing back the feeling of comfort.

Too Bad for Small Minds

Once upon a time,
not so long ago,
a man believed in fairy tales
of love and so much more;
of peace and understanding,
non-judgment and faith,
but it was all destroyed
and slowly laid to waste.
From repetitive abuse,
constant black and white lies,
fingers being pointed
in these tear-infested eyes
that suffer from the sight
of all that they have seen;
blasphemous treachery
in a world that is obscene
to the beauty that was lost,
and suffocated hope;
organized religion's just
another form of dope
for the medicated masses
that fill up this place.
this soul has been drained;
it's only taking up space
in a world that is too small,

overpopulated,
kill 'em all and fuck the rest;
we will all end up dead.